# Getting in Shape

## for Viola

by Cassia Harvey

edited by Judith Harvey

CHP 124

©2004 by C. Harvey Publications All Rights Reserved.

www.charveypublications.com - print books
www.learnstrings.com - PDF downloadable books
www.harveystringarrangements.com - chamber music

Less-advanced (A) pages are structured so that they can be played together with more-advanced (B) pages.

# Contents

| Page | | Page | |
|---|---|---|---|
| 2 | Finger Trainer (A) | 30 | Exercise for Both Hands (A/B) |
| 3 | Little Brown Jug (A) | 31 | Karobushka (A/B) |
| 4 | Finger Trainer (B) | 32 | Pre-Skipping (A) |
| 5 | Little Brown Jug (B) | 33 | Fireworks Music (A) |
| 6 | Finger Workout (A) | 34 | Pre-Skipping (B) |
| 7 | Soldier's Chorus (A) | 35 | Fireworks Music (B) |
| 8 | Finger Workout (B) | 36 | Skipping (A) |
| 9 | Soldier's Chorus (B) | 37 | Arkansas Traveler (A) |
| 10 | Daily Exercise (A) | 38 | Skipping (B) |
| 11 | The Frog Went A-Courting (A) | 39 | Arkansas Traveler (B) |
| 12 | Daily Exercise (B) | 40 | First Position Workout (A) |
| 13 | The Frog Went A-Courting (B) | 41 | High Cap (A) |
| 14 | Finger & Bow Workout (A) | 42 | First Position Workout (B) |
| 15 | Turkish Dance (A) | 43 | High Cap (B) |
| 16 | Finger & Bow Workout (B) | 44 | Pre-Skipping (A) |
| 17 | Turkish Dance (B) | 45 | Pickles for Breakfast (A) |
| 18 | Pre-Skipping (A) | 46 | Pre-Skipping (B) |
| 19 | Hopak (A) | 47 | Pickles for Breakfast (B) |
| 20 | Pre-Skipping (B) | 48 | Skipping (A) |
| 21 | Hopak (B) | 49 | Chicken on the Fence Post (A) |
| 22 | Skipping (A) | 50 | Skipping (B) |
| 23 | Brandenburg 5 (A) | 51 | Chicken on the Fence Post (B) |
| 24 | Skipping (B) | 52 | First Position Workout (A) |
| 25 | Brandenburg 5 (B) | 53 | Flower Song (A) |
| 26 | Strength Exercise (A) | 54 | First Position Workout (B) |
| 27 | Mairi's Wedding (A) | 55 | Flower Song (B) |
| 28 | Strength Exercise (B) | 56 | Skipping (A) |
| 29 | Mairi's Wedding (B) | 57 | The British Grenadiers (A) |
| | | 58 | Skipping (B) |
| | | 59 | The British Grenadiers (B) |

# Getting in Shape

## Finger Trainer (A)

Cassia Harvey

# Little Brown Jug (A)

Trad./arr. C. Harvey

# Finger Trainer (B)

Cassia Harvey

©2004 C. Harvey Publications All Rights Reserved.

# Little Brown Jug (B)

Trad./arr. C. Harvey

# Finger Workout (A)

Cassia Harvey

©2004 C. Harvey Publications All Rights Reserved.

# Soldier's Chorus (A)

Bizet/arr. C. Harvey

# Finger Workout (B)

Cassia Harvey

©2004 C. Harvey Publications All Rights Reserved.

# Soldier's Chorus (B)

Bizet/arr. C. Harvey

# Daily Exercise (A)

Cassia Harvey

# The Frog Went A-Courting (A)

Trad./arr. C. Harvey

©2004 C. Harvey Publications All Rights Reserved.

# The Frog Went A-Courting (B)

Trad./arr. C. Harvey

# Finger and Bow Workout (A)

Cassia Harvey

Getting in Shape for Viola

# Turkish Dance (A)

Kruckow/arr. C. Harvey

©2004 C. Harvey Publications All Rights Reserved.

# Finger and Bow Workout (B)

Cassia Harvey

# Turkish Dance (B)

Kruckow/arr. C. Harvey

# Pre-Skipping (A)

Cassia Harvey

©2004 C. Harvey Publications All Rights Reserved.

# Hopak (A)

Mussorgsky/arr. C. Harvey

©2004 C. Harvey Publications All Rights Reserved.

# Pre-Skipping (B)

Cassia Harvey

©2004 C. Harvey Publications All Rights Reserved.

Getting in Shape for Viola

# Hopak (B)

Mussorgsky/arr. C. Harvey

# Skipping (A)

Cassia Harvey

# Brandenburg 5 (A)

Bach/arr. C. Harvey

# Skipping (B)

Cassia Harvey

# Brandenburg 5 (B)

Bach/arr. C. Harvey

# Strength Exercise (A)

Cassia Harvey

# Mairi's Wedding (A)

Trad./arr. C. Harvey

# Strength Exercise (B)

Cassia Harvey

# Mairi's Wedding (B)

Trad./arr. C. Harvey

# Exercise for Both Hands (A/B)

Cassia Harvey

# Karobushka (A/B)

Trad./arr. C. Harvey

# Pre-Skipping (A)

Cassia Harvey

# Fireworks Music (A)

Handel/arr. C. Harvey

# Pre-Skipping (B)

Cassia Harvey

# Fireworks Music (B)

Handel/arr. C. Harvey

# Skipping (A)

Cassia Harvey

**1**

**2**

©2004 C. Harvey Publications All Rights Reserved.

# Arkansas Traveler (A)

Trad./arr. C. Harvey

# Skipping (B)

Cassia Harvey

# Arkansas Traveler (B)

Trad./arr. C. Harvey

# First Position Workout (A)

Cassia Harvey

# High Cap (A)

Trad./arr. C. Harvey

©2004 C. Harvey Publications All Rights Reserved.

# First Position Workout (B)

Cassia Harvey

Getting in Shape for Viola

# High Cap (B)

Trad./arr. C. Harvey

©2004 C. Harvey Publications All Rights Reserved.

# Pre-Skipping (A)

Cassia Harvey

©2004 C. Harvey Publications All Rights Reserved.

# Pickles for Breakfast (A)

Trad./arr. C. Harvey

# Pickles for Breakfast (B)

Trad./arr. C. Harvey

# Skipping (A)

Cassia Harvey

# Chicken on the Fence Post (A)

Trad./arr. C. Harvey

# Skipping (B)

Cassia Harvey

Getting in Shape for Viola

# Chicken on the Fence Post (B)

Trad./arr. C. Harvey

©2004 C. Harvey Publications All Rights Reserved.

# Flower Song (A)

Trad./arr. C. Harvey

# First Position Workout (B)

Cassia Harvey

# Flower Song (B)

Trad./arr. C. Harvey

©2004 C. Harvey Publications All Rights Reserved.

# The British Grenadiers (A)

Trad./arr. C. Harvey

# Skipping (B)

Cassia Harvey

©2004 C. Harvey Publications All Rights Reserved.

# The British Grenadiers (B)

Trad./arr. C. Harvey

# Available from www.charveypublications.com
# Sailing Into Bethlehem: Compatible Christmas Duets for Strings

CHP333

CHP334

CHP335